LOOKING AFTER BRITAIN

WRITTEN BY
CHRISTOPHER YEATES

COVER AND ILLUSTRATIONS BY
ZOE SADLER

© Gresham Books 2016
Published by Gresham Books Limited
The Carriage House, Ningwood Manor, Ningwood,
Isle of Wight PO30 4NJ
ISBN 978 0 946095 76 6

WHAT'S INSIDE

BRITISH VALUES

Britain is made up of England, Wales and Scotland, and the people who live in these countries are called *British*. The people of Northern Ireland may also call themselves British and together we make up the *United Kingdom*. This book is to help you learn about and come to understand some of the British Values we all share.

WHAT IS THE PUBLIC SECTOR?

Looking after Britain really means looking after the *people* of the UK, and keeping them happy. People just like you.

The *public sector* is probably the most important thing in your life you've never heard of. It provides a lot of the services that help look after the British people.

For example, the public sector provides our country with:
→ Schools and teachers.
→ Hospitals, doctors and nurses.
→ Emergency services (fire brigade, ambulance service and police).

Your life would be very different without these things – and not in a good way.

How would you feel if when you got sick, there were no doctors or nurses to look after you? What if your house was on fire, and fire engines didn't exist? What if there were no police to stop burglars from stealing all your things?

Without a system to look after Britain and its citizens, the country would be in a bit of a mess. Luckily, there is such a system. This system is called the public sector.

How is the public sector organised?

Lots of different groups of people help look after Britain. All of these groups are part of the public sector. These groups are organised by the Government of the country.

Each of the different groups provides a service which everybody in the UK can use.

These services include schools, hospitals, roads, the police, the military – and many other useful things besides.

The public sector is a lot like your body. It is a single thing, but it is made up of lots of different parts.

Each of these parts has a special job in looking after Britain, just like the different parts of your body have a special job in looking after you.

When all of these parts are working well together, better services are provided to the people of Britain.

5

What we mean when we say...

Public Sector: services provided by the Government that help look after the needs of the people. Britain's public sector includes services like providing schools, hospitals and the police.

Government: the group of people that we have chosen to lead our country.

Your turn to speak

Discuss with your partner:

→ Do you think that governments should provide services to help look after people? What kind of services do you think these should be? For example, do you think governments should provide schools, hospitals, police, roads and motorways?

→ Which of the following public sector services do you think is the most important: *schools, hospitals, collecting our rubbish, roads and motorways, police or the armed forces?*
Can you explain why?

→ Ask your teacher which public service they think is the most important and why. Do you agree?

Read and understand

1. Primary schools like yours are part of the public sector. Almost everything in your classroom has been provided for you through the public sector. Draw a picture of some of the things in your classroom that the public sector has provided for you.

2. Make a list of services that you can think of that are provided by the public sector.

3. In your own words explain what you think we mean by the public sector.

TO THE RESCUE: THE EMERGENCY SERVICES

One of the most important parts of the public sector is our country's *emergency services*. The emergency services are there to help us when we see, or are involved in, a scary, dangerous situation that we cannot deal with on our own.

The emergency services are highly-trained experts who know how to tackle even the scariest, most dangerous situation. The emergency services have two main jobs:

→ To provide care and rescue in a 999 emergency.
→ To keep us safe by helping prevent emergency situations from happening in the first place.

999 is the number you dial if you need help in an emergency. When you dial this number, you can ask for the help of:

→ Police
→ Ambulance Service
→ Fire Brigade
→ Coastguard

But it is very important that you only ever dial 999 in a real emergency.

Everyone in Britain owes a great deal to the men and women in the police, fire, ambulance and coastguard services. Every day, they risk their lives to keep all of us as safe and cared for as possible.

What we mean when we say...

Emergency Services: public services (*police, ambulance, fire brigade, coastguard*) that help people in an emergency.

Emergency: a serious, unexpected and often dangerous situation requiring immediate action.

Your turn to speak

With your partner:

→ Make a list of emergency situations that you think the emergency services could be called to.

→ It is illegal to make a hoax 999 call. Why do you think this is?

→ Why do you think our Government spends a great deal of money providing emergency services to look after us?

Read and understand

1. What telephone number should you dial in an emergency?

2. What do we mean by emergency services?

3. Describe one way that one of the emergency services might help you in an urgent situation.

THE POLICE

The police are a very important part of Britain's public sector and a key part of the country's emergency services.

The police could be called into action if:

→ There has been a serious road accident.
→ Somebody is seriously injured.
→ Somebody is feeling threatened by another person.
→ A crime has been committed, or is about to be committed.

The first thing the police will do is make the scene safe, perhaps by redirecting traffic. They then deal with the situation. This might mean making an arrest, giving first aid or organising more help from other emergency services. The police might also collect evidence from the scene, which could be used to prove whether a person has committed a crime.

Keeping us safe each day is also very important. That is why you will see police on patrol, looking out for suspicious behaviour and making people think twice before causing any trouble.

If you ever feel like something is wrong in your neighbourhood, or you want to talk about something that's worrying you, seek out your friendly local Police Community Support Officer (PCSO).

What we mean when we say...

Emergency Services: public services that help people in an emergency.

Emergency: a serious, unexpected, and often dangerous situation requiring immediate action.

Evidence: facts or information that help us work out if something is true.

Suspect: the person accused of committing a crime.

Your turn to speak

With your partner:

→ Make a list of emergency situations that you think the police could be called to.

→ What do you think it would be like to be a policeman or policewoman? Make a list of five qualities you think you would need to be a member of the police.

Read and understand

1. Collecting evidence is a very important part of police work. Try making your own fingerprint poster. You will see that everyone's fingerprints are different; this is why fingerprints make such useful evidence.

2. Why do we have police? Describe how they help look after and protect us.

You can find out lots more about the police, evidence and courts in a little book called – 'It's the Law!'

THE FIRE SERVICE

The fire service is another very important part of our public sector emergency services. The fire service is there to protect us from fire.

Firemen and women have large red fire engines to help them fight fires. Like police cars, fire engines have loud sirens and flashing lights to help them get to your side as quickly as possible.

Fire engines have:
➜ Many water hoses, which means several firefighters can try to stop the fire at once.
➜ Enough hose to stretch the length of three football fields.
➜ Several ladders which firefighters can use to rescue people trapped at the top of burning buildings.

Fires are extremely dangerous. If you see a fire always ring 999 as soon as you can.

To help keep us safe, the fire brigade also spend a lot of time going to schools, offices and people's houses to give advice on fire safety.

Fun fact: The UK's first fire brigades were formed following the Great Fire of London in 1666.

What we mean when we say...

Emergency Services: public services that help people in an emergency.

Fire Service: the group of people who protect us from fire.

Your turn to speak

Discuss with your partner:

→ What do you think it would be like to be a fireman or woman?

→ What kind of equipment does a fire engine have to help fight fires?

Read and understand

1. Draw a picture of a fire engine showing some of the equipment that firemen use to fight fires.

2. What telephone number should you dial if you need to call the fire brigade?

3. Why do you think our Government provides us with a fire service?

THE AMBULANCE SERVICE

The ambulance service is another very important part of our public sector emergency services.

The main job of the ambulance service is to provide emergency medical treatment to people who have been injured in a dangerous situation or suddenly become very ill.

There are two parts to their job:

1. To get the injured or sick person to hospital as quickly as possible.
2. To help the injured or sick person as much as they possibly can on the way to the hospital. This is usually the job of paramedics, who are specially trained in emergency first aid.

The ambulance service is often called to support the police and fire emergency officers, because dangerous situations mean it is very likely that people will need medical help.

The ambulance service sometimes uses helicopters to get to dangerous situations in remote places, such as at the top of mountains or in the middle of the countryside.

What we mean when we say...

Emergency Services: public services that help people in an emergency.

Ambulance Service: the group of people who provide emergency medical care.

Paramedic: a person trained to carry out emergency first aid but who is not a doctor.

Your turn to speak

Discuss with your partner:

→ In what kind of emergency situations would you call for an ambulance?

→ A paramedic is trained to carry out emergency first aid. What kind of person do you think you need to be, to be a paramedic?

Read and understand

1. What telephone number should you dial if you need to call an ambulance?

2. Make a fact sheet showing when you should call for an ambulance.

3. Describe the main job of the ambulance service.

4. Make your own poster showing the different services provided by Britain's three main emergency services: the Police, the Fire Service and the Ambulance Service.

WHAT A LOAD OF RUBBISH: REFUSE COLLECTORS

Many people in the public sector do very important jobs that we just take for granted, like refuse collectors. Refuse collectors, or binmen, help to look after Britain by getting rid of our waste in a safe, organised way.

If rubbish were not taken away, the streets would soon become messy and smelly, and rats and other pests would probably move in. This could all lead to some nasty diseases.

Fortunately for us, refuse collectors pick up our bins and empty them into the back of a special bin lorry called a Refuse Collection Vehicle, or RCV.

There are different types of waste that they collect:
→ Waste from people's houses.
→ Waste from people's gardens.
→ Waste which can be recycled (broken down and used again).

Many binmen collect rubbish from as many as 1600 houses and walk over 15 miles every single day. At the end of the day, the lorry returns to the depot where the RCVs are stored. At the depot, all the waste that has been collected that day is sorted into enormous, separate piles.

What we mean when we say...

Refuse: another word for rubbish.

RCV: Refuse Collection Vehicle. The special lorry used to collect and deal with your rubbish.

Recycle: use again. A lot of our rubbish can be recycled and converted into useful items.

Depot: place where things are stored.

Your turn to speak

Discuss with your partner:

→ What do you think would happen to your rubbish if we didn't have binmen to come and collect it?

→ What stages does our rubbish go through once you have left it out for collection?

Read and understand

1. How many houses does a refuse collector collect rubbish from in one day?

2. Make a poster showing what happens to our rubbish once it has been collected.

3. Explain why you think our Government provides refuse collectors to collect our rubbish. What problems might there be if our rubbish was not collected?

BUILDING AND LOOKING AFTER BRITAIN'S ROADS

Motorways, roads and lanes are all maintained for us by the public sector. Road workers play a key role in looking after Britain by providing the *infrastructure* (or framework) for cars, buses, lorries and bikes.

A country's infrastructure is extremely important. Without it we would not be able to transport food, fuel and other important supplies.

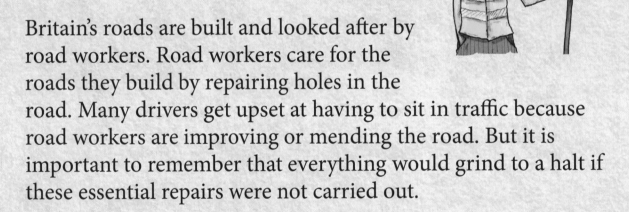

Britain's roads are built and looked after by road workers. Road workers care for the roads they build by repairing holes in the road. Many drivers get upset at having to sit in traffic because road workers are improving or mending the road. But it is important to remember that everything would grind to a halt if these essential repairs were not carried out.

Road workers also put up all the signs you see on the road which tell people how to get to the places they want to go, and paint the white marks you see which tell people which side of the road to drive on, or what speed to go at.

Fun fact: Britain has an astonishing 245,000 miles of road, which is enough to wrap around the world ten times. Ten!

What we mean when we say...

Infrastructure: a framework. Roads are an important part of a country's infrastructure.

Your turn to speak

With your partner:

→ Make a list of items that you use that will have been transported by road. (Remember everything in your local supermarket will have had to be delivered to the supermarket by road!)

Read and understand

1. What do road workers do?

2. Draw your own picture of a road traffic sign. Do you know what the sign means?

3. What is the longest road journey you have done? Why were you making this journey? Would your journey have been possible without roads?

4. Why do you think our Government provides roads and motorways for our country?

A SCHOOL EDUCATION FOR EVERY CHILD

The public sector looks after Britain by providing teachers and schools, so that every single child in the country can go to school and be educated until they are at least 16 years old.Providing an *education* for every child and young person is a very important part of the work of the public sector.

It doesn't matter whether you are a boy or a girl, what religion you follow, or how much money you have; everybody is entitled to go to school. The public sector makes sure that everyone has the opportunity to make the most of their talents and abilities, whatever they may be.

The public sector looks after Britain by making sure that everybody in the country can go to school until they are at least 16 years old.

Every school employs a great many people. These include:
+ Headteachers
+ Teachers
+ Teaching assistants
+ Librarians
+ IT experts
+ Cooks
+ Caretakers

What we mean when we say...

Education: the process of receiving schooling.

Entitled: having a right to something.

Your turn to speak

Discuss with your partner:

→ What do you think are the most important things that you have learnt at school so far?

→ What are you looking forward to learning in the future?

→ Why do you think our Government thinks it is so important that every child should benefit from going to school?

→ Discuss the different jobs that people do in your school.

Read and understand

1. Make a poster showing the ways that a child can benefit from going to your school.

2. Explain why you think it is so important for every child to have the chance to go to school.

3. Write a list of the jobs done in your school by the people who work there (see bottom of page 20).

TREATING BRITAIN: THE NHS

The National Health Service, or NHS, is one more very important way that the public sector provides for us, cares for us and keeps us safe. For your whole life, if you have a medical problem, no matter how severe, you will be looked after by the NHS.

Which part of the NHS you use depends on how badly ill or hurt you are.

Your local GP

Your local doctor is known as a General Practitioner or GP. This is because he or she knows how to treat a wide variety of medical problems.

Specialists and hospitals

If a medical problem is more complicated, the GP might send you to see a specialist in a hospital. Hospitals provide specialist medical care. They look after us when it would not be possible for us to look after ourselves at home.

Hospitals have a lot of specialist medical equipment to help look after us, like X-ray machines that can tell if you have broken any bones.

Accident & Emergency

If you have an accident, you are likely to be taken to the Accident & Emergency department. Most hospitals have an A&E department.

The NHS Army

As well as all the doctors, nurses and paramedics, there is a whole army of people who work for the NHS, helping to ensure that we are all looked after. These include cleaners, cooks, receptionists, porters, ambulance drivers, nursing assistants and many more.

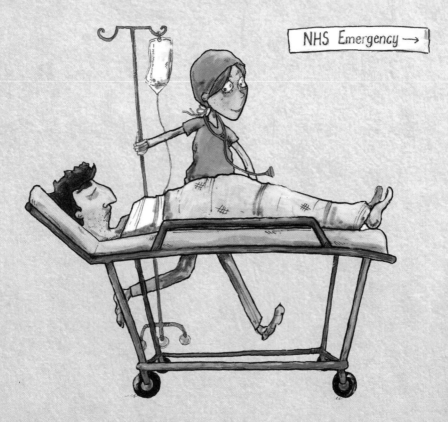

NHS Emergency →

What we mean when we say...

National Health Service: the organisation that provides free health care to Britons.

General Practitioner or GP: a doctor who treats a wide variety of medical problems, but is not a specialist.

Specialist: a doctor who has had extra training to become an expert in a particular aspect of medicine.

Your turn to speak

Discuss with your partner:

→ What kind of person do you think you need to be to become a doctor or a nurse?

→ Why do you think it is so important to be able to see a doctor or go to hospital when you need to?

Read and understand

1. What name do we use for your local doctor?

2. Which part of a hospital would you be taken to if you had an accident?

3. Make a list of the jobs of the people who work in the NHS.

4. Design a poster explaining all the benefits of the NHS.

KEEPING BRITAIN SAFE

The British Armed Forces look after the defence of our country. This might mean their being sent by our Government to fight in a war.

There are three main parts to the Armed Forces:
→   The British Army, which protects Britain on land.
→   The Royal Navy, which protects Britain at sea.
→   The Royal Air Force (often shortened to RAF), which protects Britain from the sky.

Sometimes the Armed Forces are called on to help people in times of emergency. When rivers burst their banks, you might have seen pictures on television of RAF helicopters rescuing people, or the army helping with flood defences.

Britain is also protected by its Intelligence Services, such as MI5 and MI6 – the shady world of spies and 007...

At the very top of the military's chain of command is our Monarch. Every member of the Armed Forces swears an oath of allegiance to the Monarch, but it is our elected Government which decides how the Armed Forces should be used. Only if the Government feels it is absolutely necessary will it ask the Armed Forces to fight in a war.

What we mean when we say...

The Armed Forces: Britain's military services – the British Army, the Royal Navy and the Royal Air Force.

Oath of Allegiance: a promise to be loyal.

Your turn to speak

With your partner:

→ Make a list of the different jobs done by the Armed Forces.

→ Discuss why you think our Government provides us with Armed Forces.

Read and understand

1. Draw a picture of a member of the Armed Forces.
2. What are the three main parts of the Armed Forces?
3. Who else helps to keep Britain safe?
4. Who decides whether the Armed Forces should fight in a war?

THE PRIME MINISTER AND THE CABINET

The activities of the public sector are organised by the *Cabinet*. The Cabinet is a small group of around 21 Ministers who are chosen by the *Prime Minister*.

The Prime Minister is the leader of the Cabinet. Each Cabinet Minister is in charge of one part of the public sector, called a Department.

The Minister for Health is in charge of the Department of Health, which runs the NHS. The Minister for Education is in charge of the Department for Education, which decides how our schools should be run. The Minister for Defence is in charge of the Department for Defence, which controls the Armed Forces.

Each Government Department also has lots of civil servants, who help to put the ideas and wishes of the Cabinet Minister into action. The Prime Minister usually meets with the Cabinet once a week, at Number 10 Downing Street.

What we mean when we say...

Cabinet: a committee of Government Ministers responsible for controlling how each Government Department is run.

Prime Minister: the leader of the Government, who lives at No. 10 Downing Street.

Cabinet Minister: head of a Government Department.

Civil Servant: someone who helps the Cabinet Minister run a Government Department.

Your turn to speak

Discuss with your partner:

→ If you could be a cabinet minister, which of the following parts of the public sector would you like to be in charge of? Can you explain why?

- *Education* (schools and teachers)
- *Health* (National Health Service)
- *Defence* (Armed Forces)
- *Police*
- Or would you like to be *Prime Minister*?

Read and understand

1. Draw a picture of the Cabinet meeting with the Prime Minister at Number 10 Downing Street. Remember there are around 21 Cabinet Ministers and the Prime Minister.

2. Who is in charge of the Cabinet?

3. Explain how the Prime Minister and his or her Cabinet Ministers work together to run the public sector.

WHERE DOES ALL THE MONEY COME FROM? THE BUDGET

Your parents have to manage your family's budget, and work out how much money your family has, and what you can and cannot afford to spend your money on.

In the same way, Britain's Chancellor of the Exchequer is the Government Minister responsible for running our country's budget. The Chancellor of the Exchequer has to make sure that there is enough money to pay for all of the services provided by the public sector.

The Chancellor has a very difficult job to do because each part of the public sector is very expensive and would love to have more money. But if, for example, all of the country's money went on the NHS, there wouldn't be enough for our schools or the emergency services.

The Government gets its money from the tax paid by the people. The tax that people pay provides Britain with the money to pay for everything in the public sector.

What we mean when we say...

Budget: an estimate of how much money you have to spend.

Tax: money paid to the Government by the citizens. Most people have to pay the Government some tax out of the money they earn.

Your turn to speak

Discuss with your partner:

→ Who do you think the Chancellor of the Exchequer should give most money to? Can you explain why?

- *Police*
- *National Health Service*
- *Fire Brigade*
- *Britain's infrastructure* (which includes roads)
- *Education* (schools and teachers)
- *Armed Forces*

Read and understand

1. Pretend you are the Chancellor of the Exchequer and you have to decide how to spend our country's money. Make a pie chart of how you would spend the Government's money on our public sector. Which part of the public sector would you give the biggest slice of the pie to? Decide how big a slice of the pie each of these parts of the public sector should receive:
    *   *Police*
    *   *National Health Service* (doctors, nurses and hospitals)
    *   *Fire Service* (firemen to help protect us from fire)
    *   *Britain's infrastructure* (which includes refuse collection, and building and maintaining roads)
    *   *Education* (schools and teachers)
    *   *Armed Forces* (British Army, Royal Navy & Royal Air Force)

2. Where does the money come from to pay for Britain's public sector services?

3. What does the Chancellor of the Exchequer do?

DO YOU REMEMBER?

Let's finish by reminding ourselves of some of the most important points we've learned:

→ Public sector services play a very important part in helping keep you safe. These include the Emergency Services, consisting of: *Police, Ambulance Service, Fire Brigade and Coastguard.*

→ The British Armed Forces also help protect us. The Armed Forces are made up of the British Army, the Royal Navy and the Royal Air Force.

→ One of the largest parts of the public sector is the National Health Service. The NHS provides you and your family with medical care through providing you with a GP, hospitals, specialists, nurses and all of the other people who work in a hospital.

→ The public sector provides education for every child until at least the age of 16, by making sure that there are schools and teachers.

→ Each part of the public sector is run by a Government Minister chosen by the Prime Minister. These Ministers work together in the Cabinet. The Cabinet is a committee of Government Ministers led by the Prime Minister.

→ The Chancellor of the Exchequer is the government minister in charge of the Government's money.
Taxes paid by the people pay for most of the services provided by the public sector.